*V*isiting the *P*ast

Ellis Island

Tristan Boyer Binns

Heinemann Library
Chicago, Illinois

©2002 Reed Educational & Professional Publishing
Published by Heinemann Library,
an imprint of Reed Educational & Professional Publishing,
Chicago, Illinois 60602

Customer Service 1-888-454-2279

Visit our website at www.heinemannlibrary.com

Designed by Wilkinson Design
Photographs by Tristan Boyer Binns
Illustrations by Mark Anderson
Printed and bound at Lake Book, Chicago, Illinois

06 05 04 03 02
10 9 8 7 6 5 4 3 2 1

Library of Congress Cataloging-In-Publication Data
Binns, Tristan Boyer, 1968-
  Ellis Island / Tristan Boyer Binns.
    p. cm. -- (Visiting the past)
Includes bibliographical references and index.
  ISBN 1-58810-270-X
  1. Ellis Island Immigration Station (N.Y. and N.J.)--Juvenile
literature. 2. United States--Emigration and
immigration--History--Juvenile literature. [1. Ellis Island Immigration
Station (N.Y. and N.J.) 2. United States--Emigration and immigration.]
I. Title. II. Series.
  JV6484 .B56 2001
  304.873--dc21
                                                  2001002468

Acknowledgments
The author and publisher would like to thank the following for permission to reproduce photographs
By courtesy of the National Park Service, U.S. Department of the Interior: pp. 4, 6, 9, 11, 12, 14, 17, 19,
21, 23, 25, 26.

The author and publisher would like to thank Jeff Dosik, Geraldine Santoro, and Charles Walker at Ellis
Island National Monument, and Barbara Agresti.

Special thanks to George Tselos and Barry Moreno at Statue of Liberty/Ellis Island National Monument
for their expertise, interest in, and enthusiasm for this project.

Some words in the book are shown in bold, **like this.**
You can find out what they mean by looking in the glossary.

Contents

Coming to America

In the mid-1600s, the lives of common Europeans began to change. Machines helped people farm and make goods more efficiently. But this also meant that fewer people were needed to work. People were also living longer lives. With more people, there was less work for each person. Some people suffered from **religious persecution**. The promise of work and land in the North American colonies, along with the freedom to believe in any religion, made the "New World" seem like a great opportunity.

But for a long time, North America and the United States were difficult to reach. Despite sea voyages that were long, dangerous, and expensive, people made the journey, which could take two months. Bad water, little or no food, cramped space, no toilets, and seasick people everywhere were some of the problems. When steamboats became popular in the mid-1800s, the trip took only two weeks. Conditions on board improved. Those who had enough money could sail in first- or second-class cabins.

▲ Passengers in **steerage** didn't have much space to themselves.

"Once there was a **pogrom** in our town and we had to run. I said to my mother, 'Ma, we are such good people. Why are they killing us?'"
Fannie Friedman, Ukranian Jew, 1921

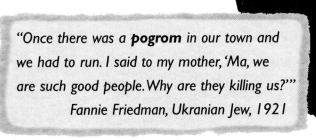

▲ This concertina—a musical instrument—came from Russia in 1909, and this small doll came from Sweden.

◀ Even the ticket for second class travel looked nicer than one for steerage.

These passengers had their own rooms and better service for the trip. But more importantly, they were allowed into the United States easily. Inspectors and doctors came to their cabins and made sure they weren't sick and then allowed them to go straight off the boat and into the United States. The **process** was different for most passengers who traveled in steerage. When they arrived, they had to go through the inspection process before they were allowed into the United States. This is why places like Ellis Island existed—to process the millions of arriving **immigrants**, making sure they were healthy and were not undesirable in any way.

▶ This steerage ticket was for passage from Palermo, Italy. During the busy years, one out of every three immigrants passing through Ellis Island was from Italy.

"I couldn't lift my head for four days. On the ship I thought I would never see the United States. I thought I would die if I went on any longer. But as we came near shore the seasickness left me."

Steve Pakan, from the former Czechoslovakia

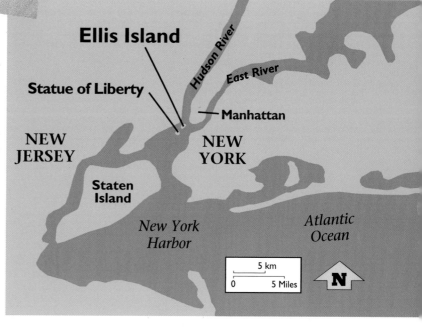

Ellis Island Beginnings

Three out of four **immigrants** coming into the United States landed in New York City. Beginning in 1855, immigrants went to a place called Castle Garden. At this time, there were no laws about who could enter the country. Only very sick or very poor people were **detained**, but everyone else could enter the country. In 1882, Congress passed the first immigration restriction law. It stated that **convicts**, mentally ill people, and those who could not support themselves would not be allowed into the United States. Later laws also made it illegal for companies to import workers from foreign countries. This was supposed to make it easier for people already living in the United States to get work. The workers at Castle Garden could not handle the added pressure of enforcing these laws. In 1890, the **federal** government decided to build a larger **processing** station in New York City.

Ellis Island was originally a small island made of soft clay and sand. Many people owned it before it was bought by the federal government in 1808 to be used as a fort. It was armed with guns and ammunition to protect New York Harbor from attacks. Years later, since there were no more threats of attack, a strong fort was no longer needed.

▼ This photo was taken in 1921. Today there are trees all along the sides of the island, and the area between Islands 2 and 3 has been filled in.

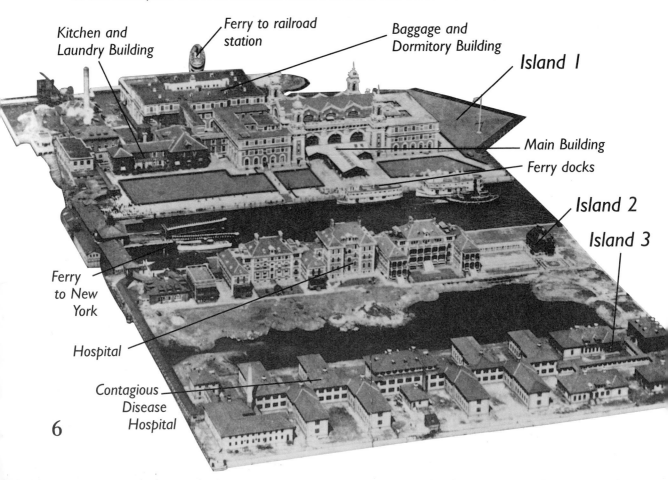

Kitchen and Laundry Building

Ferry to railroad station

Baggage and Dormitory Building

Island 1

Main Building

Ferry docks

Island 2

Island 3

Ferry to New York

Hospital

Contagious Disease Hospital

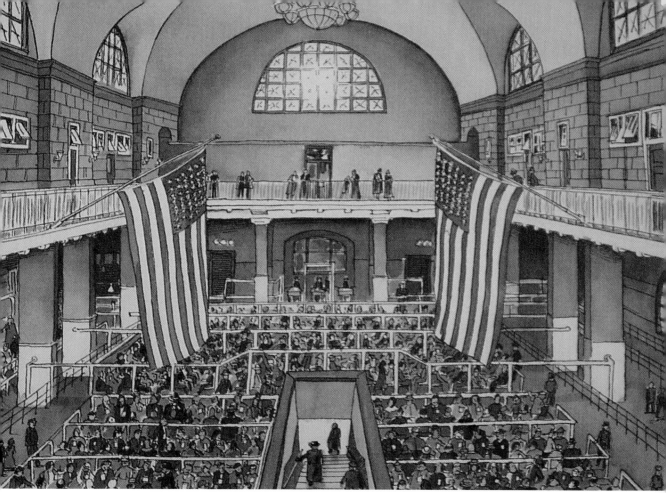

▲ People were examined by the doctors here, then waited to see the inspectors.

In 1890, the ammunition was moved off Ellis Island and construction of immigration buildings began. More immigration laws were passed in 1891, making it illegal for beggars, criminals, and others to enter the country. These laws also required ships to keep a **manifest**, or list of all passengers, which included personal information about each passenger.

The first building on Ellis Island opened in January 1892. It was made of wood, looked like a big hotel, and could handle the passage of 10,000 people each day. But on June 14, 1897, after 1,644,000 people had been processed there, it burned down in 3 hours. No one was killed, but the structure had to be rebuilt.

All new buildings were made of fireproof brick and stone.

Ellis Island now had very large waiting rooms, separate **dormitories** for men and women, a restaurant, a hospital, a baggage room, baths and laundries for **disinfecting** people and clothes, hearing rooms, and a railway and telegraph office. The size of the island was increased using **landfill** to allow larger buildings to be built.

The busiest year for immigration was 1907, when more than 1,200,000 people passed through Ellis Island. By the time it closed in 1954, more than 12 million people had been processed there.

Arriving at Ellis Island

The sea voyage was long for most **immigrants**. People were packed into small spaces below the ships' decks without much fresh air and with very little food. Many travelers became seasick. But during the journey, they kept thinking of *America,* and of the opportunity for a better life. Seeing the Statue of Liberty as they sailed into New York Harbor meant that they had reached the United States.

Big ocean liners that carried immigrants docked at piers on the Hudson River. During busy times on Ellis Island, immigrants waited on the ship for days. Then the passengers were called into line. **Processing** was done according to the ship's **manifest**. Cards with numbers were pinned to each passenger's coat. The numbered cards matched numbers in the manifest. Next, the immigrants boarded ferries and were taken to Ellis Island. On busy days at Ellis Island, the ferries had to wait hours to dock. Finally, the immigrants lined up outside the Main Building, sometimes for hours longer, waiting their turn to go in.

Many immigrants did not know about Ellis Island or the immigration process. Most who did know of Ellis Island feared it. They had heard stories of **corruption.** In the early years, some immigrants were cheated out of their money and had their possessions stolen. Reforms made in

▲ Even young children knew about the Statue of Liberty and the hope of freedom it promised the immigrants.

> *"Everybody was sad there. There was not a smile on anybody's face. Here they thought maybe they wouldn't go through. There they thought maybe my child won't go through."*
>
> Fannie Kligerman, Russian

▶ The ferries docked right in front of the Main Building.

▶ The canopy, a type of roof, once sheltered immigrants waiting to begin the process inside the Main Building. The immigrants had all their baggage with them. They could only bring what they could carry.

1902 ended this type of corruption. Also, the often changing immigration laws confused many immigrants. Some years the laws made it harder for people to enter the United States. But for most arriving immigrants, the three to five hours they spent at Ellis Island were routine, and nothing bad happened.

The baggage room was on the ground floor of the main building. This is where much of the confusion and fear began. The room was filled with families and friends trying to stay together, many speaking different languages, and few really understanding what was happening or what to do next. Many immigrants, believing that their possessions might be stolen, held on to them, crowding the room even more.

▲ Today, the canopy covers visitors to the island.

"They came with such high hopes, so much expectation. No suitcases, just a bundle of something. You saw all kinds of people, babies, all the way up. Old people. The people that had arrived from somewhere on some ship were so kind—they tried to help each other."

Irma Busch, German

◀ The baggage room was inside the main entrance. Later, it was moved to a new building behind the Main Building.

9

The Registry Room

Leaving the baggage room, **immigrants** walked up the big staircase. As soon as they started up, doctors watched them for any signs of illness. People who limped or couldn't catch their breath were suspected of having problems with their legs or having heart disease. At the top of the stairs, a doctor checked and stamped each person's card. Then the immigrants went into the registry room.

Another doctor did a head-to-toe check for mental illness, diseases, or other physical problems. Each exam took about six seconds. This doctor checked everyone's scalp for a disease called favus. The next doctor checked eyes for poor vision, **cataracts**, and especially for trachoma, an eye disease that sometimes causes blindness. This disease was very **contagious** and hard to cure. U.S. citizens and the government did not want dangerous diseases to enter the country.

▲ The registry room is huge, with a high, tiled ceiling and a balcony along the second floor.

Doctors used a piece of chalk to mark an immigrant's shoulder if problems were suspected. Doctors used letters as a code for the illnesses. "L" meant lameness; "H" meant heart disease; "Pg" meant the woman was pregnant; "Ct" meant trachoma; "E" meant eye problems; "Sc" meant favus; and "X" meant mental illness. Anyone with a chalk mark on his or her coat was taken from the main line and sent to a different room. There, doctors carefully examined the person to see if they really had the illness.

"When we arrived at Ellis Island everyone was very nervous and we passed through the lines and there were men on either side, and on some of the people those men put chalk marks on their backs. The people themselves did not know it. People in back of them could see it and were worried and wondering what it was all about."

Rachel Goldman, arrived during WW I

◀ These immigrants are having their eyes checked as part of their quick medical exams. The woman on the left has an "E" on her coat. She will be taken to a smaller room near the registry room for a more thorough examination.

Parents and children were often separated this way. Sometimes they did not know if they would meet again. Usually, separated families were reunited after a short wait. Since many families had to wait for at least a few days, **dormitories** and the big restaurant were needed.

For every ten immigrants who went through the immigration **process**, eight did not have to wait. Most immigrants were healthy. If they were not, they would not have survived the difficult trip from their homes to the United States.

▶ As immigrants came through the main door, the big staircase was directly in front of them. It was removed in 1912 because it used up too much floor space. A new staircase was put in, to the right of the old one.

◀ The big staircase came out in the middle of the registry room floor.

After passing the doctors' checks, **immigrants** went into the middle of the registry room. They sat or stood for hours, waiting to be questioned. They were organized into groups, in the order of their ships' **manifests**. At first, they were kept in metal cages, one for each group. Later, the cages were taken away and people waited on benches instead. A line of inspectors stood behind tall desks. They used information on the ship's manifest to help question each immigrant. The manifest pages had information like names, ages, birthplaces, jobs, and health. A group of **interpreters** was standing by. Inspectors looked at information from the doctors, the ship's manifest, and the immigrants to decide whether or not to allow an immigrant to enter the country. Inspectors always asked immigrants if they were married and where they planned to go in the United States.

▲ After the metal bars were removed, the registry room felt less like a cage. The inspectors waited behind desks by the stairs.

Sometimes inspectors also asked how much money an immigrant had. For a while, immigrants had to have $25 to be allowed to stay. Immigrants had to prove that they could get a job to earn money. Many had a hard time proving this, especially if they were unmarried women, children, sick, or disabled.

► This photo was taken before 1912. The big staircase still opens into the middle of the registry room. The immigrants had to wait in lines inside the metal bars as they made their way through the room.

▲ The "stairs of separation" led out from the registry room. The left side went to the railroad office and the right side went to the New York ferry. People who were detained were sent down the center stairs.

Because **convicts** were not allowed into the United States, immigrants were also asked if they had ever been in jail. They were asked what kind of job they did. Finally, they were asked if they already had a job. If they answered yes, they were not allowed into the United States. The U.S. government did not want its citizens to lose jobs to immigrants. Many new immigrants were willing to work for less money than U.S. citizens. This law did not apply to immigrants who were coming to work in a family business or had friends who promised them work. But sometimes inspectors could be hard to convince.

◄ This badge was worn by an inspector who had been an immigrant himself. He came from Poland and passed through Ellis Island in 1921. In 1930, he went to work at Ellis Island.

After 1917, immigrants had to prove that they could read in their language. If the inspectors thought that there were problems, they **detained** an immigrant for more questioning. Otherwise, the immigrants were free to go. About three to five hours after they arrived, they were free to leave Ellis Island. They went down the "stairs of separation" directly behind the inspectors' desks, and out to start their new lives in the United States.

◄ An inspector would have used a desk like this one as he questioned immigrants.

Leaving the Island

The next stop was the railway ticket office. Here there were ticket sellers and people selling food. There were also waiting rooms, a telegraph office, and a place to change money. Even without officials pushing the **immigrants** from line to line, there were still many people telling them what to do. The confusion continued as immigrants made plans to get off the island and go to their new homes. They grabbed their luggage from the baggage master's office. Some paid for it to be sent to their new homes.

At this point, all immigrants had to leave. Some unmarried people or whole families arrived without friends or family to meet them. They went to the railway office to buy tickets to travel. The major railway lines sold tickets so people could get anywhere in the country once they left Ellis Island. The ferry only went to New York City.

Many new immigrants had families expecting them. They sent **telegrams** or postcards as soon as they were through, telling their families to come meet them. Many happy families were reunited on Ellis Island.

▲ These people are buying railway tickets at the Ellis Island ticket office. The woman still has her card pinned to her jacket.

▼ When Friede Goldflusz arrived from Russia, she sent a telegram to a relative asking to be met at Ellis Island.

► These are some of the trunks and bags immigrants carried to America. One is labeled from Bremen, in Germany.

◀ Immigrants took a short ferry ride to the railroad station. This station isn't used any more.

railroad station

Ellis Island

ferry dock

▶ The ferry to New York City left from the dock near where the immigrants docked when they first arrived.

"I waited for my father, but he never came. I was upset because other people were leaving. And because I couldn't get off Ellis Island, because … I was a **minor**. But he came the next morning."
Samuel Silverman, Austrian, 1913

Unmarried women and children were not allowed off the island until a husband or father came and claimed them, or until they had a telegram saying someone would be waiting for them at their final destination. They waited in the **dormitories** until then.

At this point in the process, people were hungry. There were stands selling box lunches and snacks for 50¢ to $1. Immigrants usually bought a sandwich, fruit, and pie. To buy food, immigrants had to have U.S. money. They arrived with the money from their countries, which had to be changed into U.S. dollars.

Private companies ran these services, not the government. Over the years, some companies cheated immigrants. Some railways would send people on longer routes to make more money. Food sellers overcharged people for food. The money changers charged too high a fee or didn't make fair exchanges. When William Williams took charge of Ellis Island in 1902, he tried to stop the cheating.

Forced to Stay

About two out of every ten **immigrants** who passed through Ellis Island were **detained**, or held there. That is almost two and a half million people. There were many reasons to be detained. Sometimes immigrants arrived too late in the day to be inspected. They stayed the night and started the process the next morning. Many were held for a short time after they were inspected, waiting for family or friends to pick them up or send them money.

Some people were detained after talking with inspectors. If an immigrant had no money, seemed too weak to earn a living, couldn't read, or had once been in jail, he or she had a hard time getting past the inspectors. These immigrants waited to be heard by a **Board** of Special Inquiry, which decided if they would be sent back to where they had come from. About 2 percent of all the people who came to Ellis Island were **excluded.**

"I remember the unhappiness of the people that couldn't stay. I mean, the crying and the sadness. The huddling together of these families that apparently were going to be sent back, or kept at Ellis Island for a few days."
Lara Bisset, French, 1920

▲ This room was also used for medical testing. The floors and part of the walls were tiled to make cleaning easier.

► While people waited for more medical testing, they sometimes wrote on the walls.

◄ The Polish immigrant who had this inspection card left Danzig, Poland, on November 20, 1925. He was detained on Ellis Island and sent to the hospital on December 4, 1925.

Anyone with a chalk mark on his or her shoulder from a doctor was held in a special area. Here, another doctor decided if the person was really sick. Men and women were put in separate rooms. Then doctors examined them closely. Any children who were detained had their temperatures taken every day. This helped to keep those who were sick away from the healthy.

There were hospitals on the island where sick people stayed until they were better. People were also detained if they were thought to be mentally ill. While the sick person was in the hospital, the rest of the family often waited on the island. They didn't get much news about their sick relative, so it was a hard time for them to wait and worry.

> "We were detained at Ellis Island for two weeks, because my mother and father had problems with their eyes, and they took them into the hospital, and we were left to care for ourselves. Except I had my older brother, Albert, to help out, but at night he had to go with the men, so I took care of the three, my little brother and the two sisters. But it was very lonely without our parents for two weeks. We didn't see them at all. We knew that they were in the hospital, and that's about all."
>
> Jeanne Assidian, Turkish, 1922

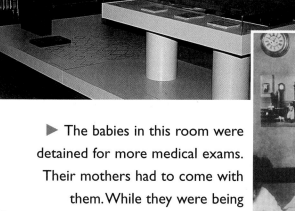

◀ Immigrants who were suspected of having mental disabilities were taken to this room and tested. The picture on the left shows some of the immigrants tested here. The one on the right shows an inspector testing an immigrant.

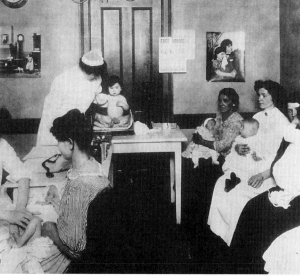

▶ The babies in this room were detained for more medical exams. Their mothers had to come with them. While they were being examined, the nurses and doctors also gave advice to their mothers about baby care in the United States.

Ellis Island Hospitals

There were also special hospitals on Ellis Island. The first was built on a new part of the island, called Island 2. Dirt removed from the digging of the New York City subway tunnels was used to build this island. Island 2 was attached to the main island by a walkway. It opened in 1902, but it was already too small by the time it opened. Even though it was added onto twice, it was never large enough.

A second hospital was built for patients with **contagious** diseases. It opened in 1911 in another new part called Island 3.

Most of the patients were children who caught diseases on their ocean journey or while waiting on Ellis Island. It had separate buildings for people with measles, scarlet fever, diphtheria, and other common diseases. Measles was the most common contagious disease. Most people who were hospitalized on Ellis Island remember the hospital staff as kind and helpful. The nurses and doctors helped children learn English, played with them, read stories to them, fed them good food, and celebrated when they got better. The families of these patients were not allowed

"Some people hate Ellis Island. I couldn't hate it. Even though they kept me there [in the hospital], I wasn't mistreated. We could play outside. We'd play ball, play tennis, and the food was good. The library was good. Once a week, you'd go to the movies. Who could go to the movies once a week in Sicily, you know?"

John Titone, Sicilian, 1920, kept in the hospital as a boy

◄ This medical testing room on the second floor by the registry room has stairs down to the first floor. They lead to a door out to the hospital on the next island.

Island 3   filled in area   Island 2

◀ Islands 2 and 3 were separate at first, but later the water in between them was filled to make a lawn area for recovering patients.

to visit much, sometimes only five minutes a week. Most patients spent between one and two weeks in the hospital.

Immigrants with diseases that could not be cured, or with physical problems that would keep them from earning a living, were usually **excluded.** A parent had to go back with a child who was excluded.

▲ People in the registry room could look out the windows to see the hospital on the next island.

Between 1900 and 1954, about 3,500 people died on Ellis Island, and about 1,400 of those were children. In that same time, more than 355 babies were born on the island. Their mothers made the journey while pregnant and gave birth to them soon after arrival.

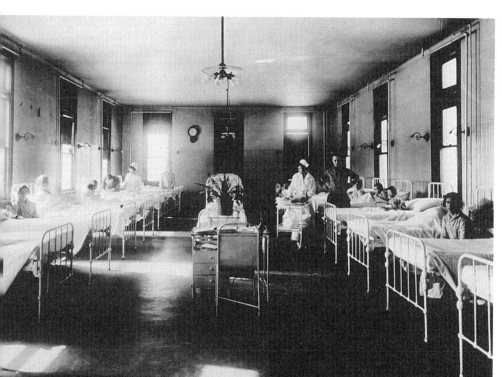

◀ This hospital photograph was taken to print in newspapers, so it was carefully posed. The room is bright and clean. Nurses, a doctor, and an orderly are helping patients.

19

Detention Rooms

Immigrants detained at Ellis Island for any reason other than sickness spent time in the detention rooms. These rooms were often so overcrowded that people felt caged, like animals. Sometimes, more than 2,500 people were kept in a place that was built to hold only 1,500. Immigrants from many different countries lived alongside each other. With so many different languages being spoken, it was a confusing place to be.

Immigrants, their possessions, and the detention rooms all got very dirty. The immigrants had not had a chance to bathe or clean their things well. They had a **disinfecting** bath when they arrived, and their clothes were cleaned to get rid of lice, but this only helped a little. Bedding and clothing quickly became filthy again. Everyone in detention had to have a shower every three days, but bodies and hair were never really clean for long.

Main Building

Baggage and Dormitory Building

◀ The Baggage and Dormitory Building next to the Main Building was finished in 1909, but it was changed many times over the years. The first floor was used for baggage and the railway offices, and the second floor was all **dormitories.**

"You didn't feel like you were free. They treated you like prisoners."
Gustav Glaser, Danish, 1924

▶ Detention rooms lined the balcony above the registry room. Later, the new Baggage and Dormitory Building was built to provide more space for the detained immigrants.

◀ Before the third floor was added to the Main Building, detained immigrants went to the rooftop for fresh air. Today, the research library's reading room sits above the rooftop.

▼ People in detention often drew graffiti on the walls, like this picture of the ship the immigrant sailed on.

Detained immigrants spent their time in several different rooms. During the days, they waited in the detention rooms. Here they sat and wrote letters home or played or talked. The walls of the rooms were created with graffiti. People wrote where they came from and how they felt waiting to get into the United States. Many immigrants spent some of their time praying.

Children played on a playground. Adults went to the rooftop for fresh air. But even the rooftop was fenced with wire so people could not escape before being completely inspected according to the law. Immigrants felt differently about their time in detention, depending on how they were treated and what stories they had heard. Many were very worried about getting into the United States or about the health of a child. Organizations like the **Salvation Army** and Hebrew Immigrant Aid Society helped explain what was happening. They also gave Passover **seders**, Christmas celebrations, and concerts.

> "It was very sad, very painful, because I was so close and yet I was so far."
> Endre Bohem, Hungarian, 1921

◀ These children had parents in detention. After 1900, detained children went to school. They were also weighed and measured because doctors wanted to keep information about immigrants.

21

Eating and Sleeping

Detention rooms became **dormitories** at night. Many people packed into the rooms, which were then locked. Bunk beds flipped down from metal bars in two or three layers from floor to ceiling. They were made of wire or canvas slung between metal frames. They were hard because they did not have mattresses. **Immigrants** were supposed to get two blankets, but these usually had lice in them so people slept with their clothes on for warmth. Some immigrants slept on the floor or on benches, because there were not enough bunks.

▼ The dining room for the immigrants was in the Kitchen and Laundry Building. It also had laundry and shower rooms. In 1915, the Bakery and Carpentry Building was finished behind it.

Bakery and Carpentry Building   Kitchen and Laundry Building

For a while, each bunk had a wire cage around it. The cages were supposed to keep the immigrants and their things safe, but they made people feel trapped. Until the 1920s, men slept in one room and the women in another. Later, when fewer people came through Ellis Island, families stayed together in private rooms.

"I have seen many jails, some pretty bad, but I never saw a jail as bad as the dormitories at Ellis Island."
Henry H. Curran, Commissioner of Immigration, 1920s

▶ The early dormitory rooms had wire bunks that flipped down at night. Many dormitory rooms also had sinks and toilets.

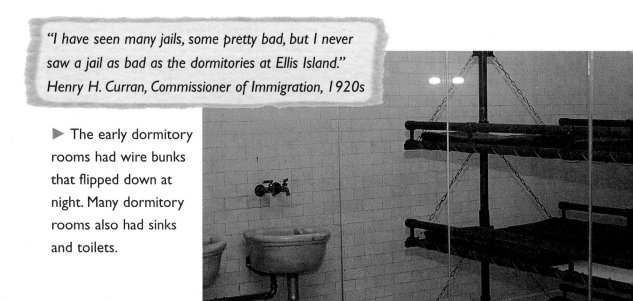

Most of the time, the dining room served foods such as coffee, oatmeal, white bread, milk, stews, boiled vegetables, and stewed fruit. Unfamiliar "American" foods, like corn on the cob and ice cream, were treats for many immigrants. Many were puzzled by bananas since they had never seen them before. Sometimes people tried to eat them without peeling them!

Many people were confused by the food, and thought it was terrible. Some could not eat the food because of their religions. Until a **kosher** kitchen opened in 1911, Jewish immigrants went hungry. Some Muslims ate only boiled eggs.

At first, the kitchens and dining room were dirty and the food *was* very bad. But it was cleaned up when William Williams took over, and by 1922, some people thought it was the cleanest room in the building. More than 1,200 people sat in the dining room at once, and all had china plates, silverware, and paper tablecloths.

▲ The china plates and silver utensils used in the dining room were made especially for Ellis Island. The plates have a picture of the island on them, and the forks have the words *Ellis Island*.

▼ This stained coffee cup was found buried in the ground when **renovations** began on the island.

◄ The dining room is packed with immigrants in this photograph.

23

Board of Special Inquiry

In the United States, anyone who is accused of a crime gets a trial by jury with a lawyer to help explain and plead his or her case. On Ellis Island, anyone **detained** and threatened with **exclusion** went in front of a **Board** of Special Inquiry. These boards were not courts. They were run by inspectors to decide if **immigrants** could enter the country or not. Immigrants could not have lawyers to help them and could not talk with friends or family before their cases were heard. The boards were made up of three inspectors, an **interpreter,** and someone to write down the decisions.

▲ Boards of Special Inquiry met in rooms like this one. Three people sat behind a long desk and heard the immigrants' cases.

The boards tried to find out if the immigrants could take care of themselves once they were living in the United States. The U.S. government did not want to be responsible for caring for sick people or paying for food and shelter for poor people. Some immigrants had a hard time convincing the board to let them in. These included immigrants who did not have money, seemed like they might not get a job, were very weak, had a physical problem, or were sick.

During the hearing, board members asked the immigrant questions. The immigrant told his or her story. Friends and family could talk about why the immigrant should be allowed into the United States.

▶ Those detained and thought to be likely to escape saw visitors from behind the screens in these walls.

▶ Immigrants waited to talk about their cases with the board from behind wooden railings.

About two out of every ten immigrants who had a case heard by the board were not let into the United States. If the board decided not to let the immigrant in, he or she could **appeal** his or her case to higher **federal** officers in Washington, D.C.

About 50 to 100 immigrants went before the board every day, so most did not have to wait long to have their cases heard. But the appeals sometimes took months. All that time, the immigrant and his or her family waited in detention. If the appeal was rejected, the immigrant was usually excluded. Many families were split up, and hopeful people trying to start new lives in the U.S. were ordered back to the countries they had left. Often, they had spent all their money getting to the United States, so they arrived back home broke.

◀ Two immigrants, standing to the right, are being questioned by Robert Watchorn, second from the left, who was in charge of Ellis Island at the time.

The Later Years

Ellis Island was usually very crowded, as more and more people came to the United States. In 1907, more than one million people passed through. But there were quiet years. During World War I, from 1914 to 1918, the Atlantic Ocean wasn't safe to cross because of possible attacks by German submarines. Only 141,390 people came to Ellis Island in 1916. **Immigrants** who were supposed to be **excluded** had to be **detained** on the island. German sailors captured in the war were also held on Ellis Island. Later, the island was used as a hospital for wounded American soldiers.

By the end of World War I, government officials were afraid that immigrants with **radical political** ideas would try to change the way Americans thought about politics and society. There was a "Red Scare," when immigrants were questioned closely and many people were **deported.**

▼ The hospital buildings are falling apart today. This is how one room looks, with peeling paint and broken furniture. Some day the hospitals may be **renovated**.

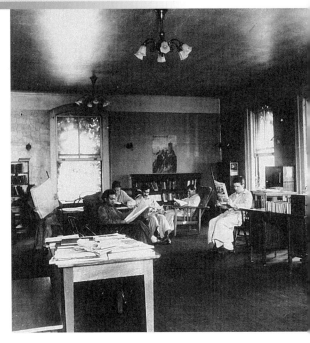

▲ These WW I soldiers are recovering from wounds in the Ellis Island hospital. This photo was taken in 1919, a year after the war had ended.

▲ The Baggage and **Dormitory** Building is also falling apart. The outside has been fenced off. Much work is needed before this building can be visited again.

▶ The baggage room in the Main Building holds an exhibit on people moving to the United States. Students often visit to learn about immigration for school projects.

After the war ended in 1918, the number of arriving immigrants increased. Many Europeans wanted to come to the United States to escape the destruction and hard times in Europe as a result of the war. The U.S. government did not want too many immigrants, so it passed the First Quota Act in 1921. Only a certain number of immigrants could come from each country each month.

In 1924, the National Origins Act became law. It lowered the numbers of immigrants allowed in from each country. This law allowed immigrants to pass inspections before they left their home countries. So when they arrived in the U.S., they did not need to stop at Ellis Island. Some people were still held there, and sick sailors were treated at the hospital.

During World War II, from 1939 to 1945, Ellis Island once again held prisoners of war. The Coast Guard also used the island as a training site. After the war, Ellis Island was used to hold immigrants with radical political opinions again. But by 1954, the island was used very little. It closed down when the immigration detainees were moved to New York City.

Over the years, the buildings on Ellis Island began to fall apart. Records and artifacts were lost. In 1965, Ellis Island became part of the Statue of Liberty National Monument. Repairs were done to make it safe again, and in 1976 visitors were allowed on the island. Between 1982 and 1990, more than $170 million were spent to restore the main island buildings. Now, more than two million visitors come each year to see Ellis Island, where so many people began new chapters in their lives.

▲ Behind the Main Building, an exhibit called the Wall of Honor has been built. People can pay to have the names of their immigrant **ancestors** carved into the wall.

Time Line

1890	Ellis Island chosen for new immigration station
January 1, 1892	Ellis Island opens
June 15, 1897	Wooden buildings all burn down
December 17, 1900	New brick and stone buildings open
March 1902	First hospital opens on Island 2 and is connected to the main island by a walkway
1902	William Williams takes over as commissioner of immigration and cleans up most of the **corruption**
1906	Robert Watchorn is commissioner of immigration
1907	Busiest year ever—more than 1 million immigrants arrive
1909	William Williams once again is commissioner of immigration until 1913
1911	Hospital for **contagious** diseases opens on Island 3
1914	World War I begins in Europe, immigration numbers drop to 178,416
1916	German submarine blows up barges in New Jersey a mile away—doors, windows, and roofs broken on Ellis Island
1918	U.S. War and Navy Departments take over Ellis Island
1920	Number of immigrants increases, more than 250,000 arrive
June 3, 1921	First Quota Act goes into effect
1924	National Origins Act becomes law. Immigrants can now be inspected before leaving their countries. Ellis Island arrivals slow to a trickle.
1954	Ellis Island immigration center closes
1965	Ellis Island is made part of Statue of Liberty National Monument
1976	Ellis Island reopens to visitors but buildings are falling apart
1982-1990	Main buildings are restored
1990	Newly renovated Ellis Island opens

Site Map

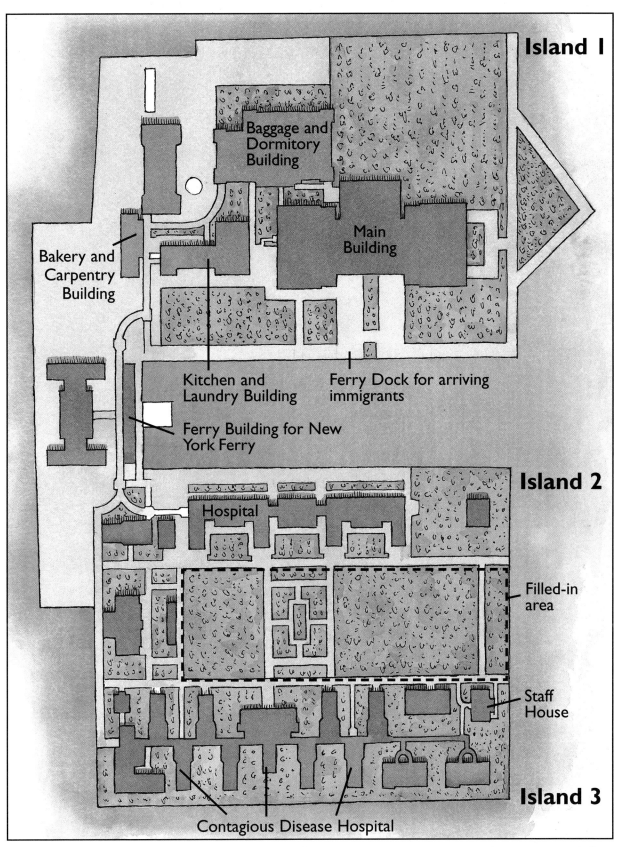

Island 1

Baggage and Dormitory Building

Main Building

Bakery and Carpentry Building

Kitchen and Laundry Building

Ferry Dock for arriving immigrants

Ferry Building for New York Ferry

Island 2

Hospital

Filled-in area

Staff House

Contagious Disease Hospital

Island 3

Glossary

ancestor someone who comes earlier in a family, such as a great-grandparent

appeal to ask a higher court to review a lower court's decision

board group of people that has managerial or other powers

cataracts condition in the eye in which the lens gets cloudy, causing poor vision

contagious easily spread from person to person

convict person who has been found guilty of a crime

corruption when things are done in a dishonest or illegal way

deported to have been officially forced to leave a country after being allowed in

detain hold or keep someone back

disinfect make clean by killing germs

dormitory building with many rooms and beds for people to live or sleep in

excluded to be kept out out of a country upon arrival

federal central part of government

immigrant person who comes to a country to live and make a new home

interpreter person who understands two or more languages and helps communicate between people who do not speak the same language

kosher fit to eat according to the Jewish laws of diet

landfill dirt and soil taken from one area and placed in another area

manifest list of passengers on a ship

minor person under the age of eighteen

pogrom organized killing of helpless people

processing going through a set of steps towards an end result

radical politics political beliefs that are not shared by a large number of other people in society

religious persecution to treat in a cruel way because of someone's religious beliefs

renovate to make new or like new

Salvation Army international religious and charity organization

seder special Jewish dinner held during Passover, a special feast

steerage section of a ship for passengers paying the lowest fares

telegram coded electrical message sent through telegraph wires, used before people had telephones

More Books to Read

Bierman, Carol. *Journey to Ellis Island: How My Father Came to America.* New York: Hyperion, 1998.

Lawler, Veronica. *I Was Dreaming to Come to America: Memories from the Ellis Island Oral History Project.* Madison, Wis.: Turtleback Books, 1997.

Quiri, Patricia Ryan. *Ellis Island.* Danbury, Conn.: Children's Press, 1998.

Stein, R. Conrad. *Ellis Island.* Danbury, Conn.: Children's Press, 1992.

Temple, Bob. *Ellis Island: Gateway to Freedom.* Chanhassen, Minn.: The Child's World, Inc., 2000.

Index